Stian Koxvig is a Norwegian writer who has been living in the UK for over three years to get away from the snow. He has Aspergers Syndrome and is very interested in mental health which caused him to compose this poetry collection about feeling alone and misunderstood in a very normal world.

To my mum. For always believing in me and my writing, for always being supportive and helping out when I didn't believe in myself.

Stian Koxvig

A DIFFERENT VIEW

AUSTIN MACAULEY PUBLISHERS™

LONDON • CAMBRIDGE • NEW YORK • SHARJAH

A CIP catalogue record for this title is available from the British Library.

ISBN 9781398426818 (Paperback)
ISBN 9781398426825 (Hardback)
ISBN 9781398426832 (ePub e-book)

www.austinmacauley.com

First Published 2023
Austin Macauley Publishers Ltd®
1 Canada Square
Canary Wharf
London
E14 5AA

I: Broken

I used to think I was a God
Untouched by emotions, feared by the Dark
And look at me now. A Broken madman
Struggling to find, the meaning of life

I used to lie to protect my heart
Manipulate and cheated my way out of Love
Only once I have broken my stone-cold heart
Maybe I should give it a new chance?

I am just a slave, to the vicious hand of time
Playing through my game, a prelude pantomime
Sitting in the shadow of my twisted mind
Am I past the point of no return?

II: The Corners of My Mind

It's not about you
It's just about me
The destroyed hope
My shattered dreams

Wake me up from this god-forsaken dream
The end of all life, the shadows of Death
The robber of Christ's wrath
Now it's time to finally realise, that we are all
Deaf dumb and blind!

The words of the writer has lost all its meaning
Insignificant words scribbled in ink
Lost in his dreams, his music, and curse
The hope of true happiness, shattered like glass
With a smile on your face, you walk him to his grave

III: The Crime

I'm not the man I once was
The large shock did change me much
Now I'm all alone and I'm about to fall
Into the shadows

I never thought it would end like this
My crime would catch me up like this
I'm ready to pay, for the crimes I've done
And I'm ready to offer my life for my sins

My conscience haunts my dreams at night
I live in shadows and seek the light,
The darkness is here and ready to fight
I'm seeking power, and I'm seeking might

The end is near
The darkness is here
And I'm filled with fear
They'll take my life, but I know it's fair

IV: Eternal

Through all your life it has been said
There comes a time to join the dead
Admit you've used your final Chance
And join Death in our final dance

The devil in the darkened skies
With a stone-filled heart filled with despise
Will take the girl, away from here
Caught in a waltz, with the eternal dancer
He fills the rest of your life with fear.

Across the fiery fields of hell
When the Devil's got you in his shell
He's in the dark to kiss your hand,
Accept that it is time to DIE!

V: The Tears of The Dragon

She is sitting there, with a gun in her hand
The tears of the dragon, was crushed to sand
Now her memory fades, across the land
Life can be hard, when you're fighting with flames

She has killed many angels, she has fought many wars
Her hatred grew stronger, and her heart became stone
She's living in shadows, and searching for light
When the darkness appears, are you ready to fight?

The tears of a dragon, burning like a flame
Life can be hard; can you deal with the shame?
It will crush you like a storm wind
No matter if you're big and strong
The tears of a dragon will always live on

She's lost in a dream, and she cannot wake up
In love with the devil, his shadow she trusts
Her powers are fading, and so is her life
The tears of the dragon, fading away

The tears of a dragon, burning like a flame.
Life can be hard; can you deal with the shame?
It will crush you like a storm wind
No matter if you're big and strong
The tears of a dragon will always live on.
The tears of a dragon, Always lives on.

VI: Blazing Dragons

I'm riding through furious pain
Covering my memories in shame
Dragons with glory
Fighting the furious flame

We have found the graves
But we're still in need of their names
I'm done playing their games
We're fighting the flames

Dragons blazing through the air
Angels crying heaven's tear
They will fight you if you dare
Blazing Dragons

The power of angels making you happy
The power of the demons seeking you dead
I'm stuck in the middle, unsure of my path
With the help of the dragons, I'm gonna survive

Dragons blazing through the air
Angels crying heaven's tear
They will fight you if you dare
Blazing Dragons

Dragons and Angels must unite
For the power of Satan is way out of hand
Blazing Angels Blazing Dragons
Darkness watch out, we're on our way

VII: The Abyss

A bubbling source of
Sugar and salt
I am chained to the stories
Of the shadows of the past

I am a lonely star
Among curious souls
But the glowing music carries tones so pure
Here grows the mysterious lily

Can you see the leaves of grass?
Of sour green emerald
Can you feel the burning heart?
By the sight of the Eternal Flame

My Mind is searching and looking
For strength sorrow and joy
How can you handle the dream I am searching?
Far away from the abyss of wrath

VIII: The Power of Love

Innocent tears are falling from the sky.
I love you so much, I just wanna cry.
I know it won't happen, so my love to you is killing me.
I'm a black ancient warrior, you are my life.

The power of love is searching the sky.
Looking down upon the warrior, who just want to die.
The sorrow grows deeper, like knifes in my breaking heart.
I'm strong like a lion, ready to fall.

I've always been a survivor.
A strong human being, alone in the dark.
I've always been a lonely wolf, then you came into my life.
You are my drug.
The Power of Love
I Love You

Every time you smile, I feel so happy.
Your pretty face, and beautiful smile.
Makes my life worth living.
And you know that I'm here. No matter what.
I always stay by you.

I've always been a survivor.

A strong human being, alone in the dark.

I've always been a lonely wolf, then you came into my life.

You are my drug.

The Power of Love

I Love You

I'll Always love you baby.

And right now I'm crying in the night.

But you are still my friend.

I'll Always be here for you.

The Power of Love

I Love You

I've always been a survivor.

A strong human being, alone in the dark.

I've always been a lonely wolf, then you came into my life.

You are my drug.

The Power of Love

I Love You

IX: To Old Age

Hey you!
Time goes by fast, people change, places die
I see you sitting near the river spreading out into the big sea
Thoughtful and wondering what tomorrow brings
Do you jump?

X: Narcissism

Only you can understand you and people like you.
Like I understand me.

XI: The Winter Song

The winter is knocking on my door
The blanket of ice falls over the fire
The cold bites us
All around us die

A simple leaf left in the snow
Alone and abandoned in the big wide world
A crystal left on the leaf
The Winter Song

You walk alone
No one can walk with you
Everything withers
Where you put your feet everything dies
The Winter Song

XII: Virginity

Say bye bye bye
Goodbye your childish mind
Prince Charming waiting for you tonight
To see your blushing smile
Dancing there in fields of wind
A yellow ribbon in your hair

Have you ever heard his name?
Without beginning to smile
So ask him up to dance tonight
And slowly untie
The yellow ribbon in your hair

XIII: Incomplete

Life is like a large symphony
You sing the same line, over and over again
There is a lot that can happen, it is a scary fairy tale
Do you know the last verse, of this incomplete life?

You can spend all your life, trying to remember words
Or enjoy the melody you made many year ago
All the words and memories, taste so sweet
So why do you insist, on hiding it away?

You can spend your whole life, trying to break free
Or live every single day on repeat
But if you can break free from the circle of life
You have to sit down, and break the chains

Life is a grand symphony
You sing all the same notes, over and over again
But to live life, for everything it is worth
You have to put a stop and wake up

XIV: The White Pearl

I was raised by the Oceans
Raw beautiful powers
I learned to stay away from
The Darkness of Mankind

The Waves are risen over my head
My home on the bottom of the sea
You used to have a home here
So very long ago

Every Night I see her in my dreams
The White Pearl
Every Night her memory returns
The White Pearl

The Graves of the Dragons
You show the way for those who need to see the light
Let's board her one last time
She will fly

There was a man who was saved from the Black Sea
Nameless and afraid

With blood on his hands
He changed their lives forever

You are the Light of the Night
Showing us the way
The Goddess of the Sea loves her complex irony

The King of the Twilight
Thrown off your throne
The Usurper from nowhere
Still have a part to play
In this forgotten world

Every night I see her in my dreams
The White Pearl
Every Night, her memory returns
The White Pearl

On the ship there is a child
Abandoned and alone
Afraid of her own magic power
That no one has seen before
Now she needs a guiding light
To show her on her path

I hope I one day will get to see
The waves of the Black Ocean
Swallow The White Pearl and me
Together till the end

XV: The Mask of Ice

The dream of the end is the secret of life
The shadows of eternity like the music of the night
Love is the music and hate is the life
And death is the sorrow edge of a knife

My identity remains under the mask of ice
Camouflaged by hatred, sorrow death and vice
A heart without a meaning to fear the so called life
The blood soaked tears of vengeance, break my mask of ice
Covered in filth of the writers beforehand
Writing lyrics with their blood, soaked in my own mind
Life is just a sad lone game and we're all players avoiding
shame
Trapped under the mask of ice

My identity remains under the mask of ice
Camouflaged by hatred, sorrow death and vice
A heart without a meaning to fear the so called life
The blood soaked tears of vengeance, break my mask of ice

The bolero of fire and the serenade of hate
Are all that remains after centuries of pain
The lake filled with blood across the dried up desserts of death
The coveted wind betrayed by the Gods.

XVI: Bloodstained Revenge

I'm sitting here in my cold wet cell
Soaked in your blood
I'm driven out of my mind
The flames of hell, burning through the poet's heart
He has realised that life is hard.
When angels and demons are drifting away
From the shame called life, and the love called hate

What's the meaning of life, when it's all filled with hate?
Sorrow, hatred, depression.
IT'S LIFE!
You may think you're so special. Have you ever felt pain?
It's a hard and heavy game, with just one single rule
SURVIVE

You only have one chance, it can easily go to despair.
Yeah I know I am crazy, everyone is!
Life can be compared to a game of Russian roulette
Yeah I know I am crazy, everyone is!

What's the meaning of life, when it's all filled with hate?
Sorrow, hatred, depression.
IT'S LIFE!
You may think you're so special. Have you ever felt pain?
It's hard and heavy game, with just one single rule

XVII: Lies

Because you whispered in my ear
I betrayed my friend
Only because my heart was
Wrapped around your finger again

Neither word nor action
Will help or forgive
Her heart is filled with pain now
And I'm alone again

XVIII: Peace

Is it real or is it a dream?
Our ability to reach ideal Peace
Is it real or is it a dream?

The world is a beautiful place
Filled with love, joy hope and peace
Daily we hear of sorrow, war and hate
The world is a horrible place

I often hear old men say
Everything was better before
One by one they fall
Down near the river
I hear the old men say
Everything was better before

XIX: The Lotus and the Willow

Down near the river
In the dark forests of the college
He used to sit and think
About his childhood days

He used to tell me daily
That there is a fine line between solitude and being lonely
Like the Lotus and the Willow
We were never meant to be

Now he is back again
Near the dark river
This time to bury her
And the Willow is weeping

Like all the Children of Time
Says goodbye to each other
He is left there all alone
Like the willow he weeps
Like the Lotus withers

His life is like an evil destiny
Filled with light and darkness
She always found the light in him
And sacrificed believing in him

XX: To You!

Hey you!
Stranger on the street
With a unique story to deal
Stop me
I will listen
Gladly

XXI: The Melodies of Life

Music
Pretty and sweet
Sounding Melodic
As if the Angels are singing
If Only I Were in Heaven
So I could hear it

XXII: I Love You

I Love You!
Three simple words that scares us all
Love is weak and ready to fall.
Hate and sorrow awaits your call
Three simple words that scares us all
I Love You

XXIII: The Last Breath of Love

You have the wings of a fallen angel
You would betray every man on earth
You live your life, killing every love you have
Watch out. Revenge will come!

You are the gift of my pathetic life
You offer me peace, and a chance to change
But dear P, can't you see it's not easy to be me
I'm an artist, my love. I paint with blood

The power you have is strange and incredible
The tragic story of love. The beauty and the beast
Can I live without you? Are you able to see through my eyes?
I have resigned us both to death
You walk me to the slaughter. Is that a smile on your face?

You have killed too many angels
Now you must face the fact and confront the truth
You have come to see the healer. And now you are afraid
To conquer all your challenges, and fight against the rage

The kiss in the rain will I always remember
You are my angel. Through fire and flames
Remember why you still live? And our pact from the past
Remember P: Pacta sunt Servanda

The power you have is strange and incredible
The tragic story of love. The beauty and the beast
Can I live without you? Are you able to see through my eyes?
I have resigned us both to death
You walk me to the slaughter. Is that a smile on your face?

The last breath of love is coming to an end
If you kill me P, you'll die too
I may be a liar. I may be an angel
You saw through my alter ego. You loved the true G

Miss Judas, I'm now on your tail
This third time we'll meet. I'm not gonna fail
I was wrapped on your little finger. Like a dog on a chain!
I stay awake this night. We'll meet the end together

XXIV: The Usurper's Confession

When the heart is stabbed with the dark thoughts of sorrow
When the blood turns black from the hatred of fear
When the angels are crying the blood tears of heaven
Your heart will rot; it's the power of death

A human's heart, more vulnerable than glass
The power of hate will tear it apart.
The angels are singing the sad hymn of grief
The demons are laughing; it feeds on your soul

Life is just a lonely game
With sad lone souls feeling shame
What's the meaning of life? What's the meaning of love?
You are a dame without a heart, not allowed to feel human
feelings

Ladies and gentlemen, please enter his life again
The sad story without an end makes you wanna kill yourself
His eyes filled with hate, and his heart turned to dust
Is there something called love? Or just hate in disguise

He had a meeting with the angels that just wished to see him happy
He had the influence of the demons, his heart like stone.
He had all the life against him, what the hell should he do?
With a knife in his hand, his true story ends.

XXV: The Fall of Avalan

You see the world in anger
I see the world in Pain
As far as the eyes can see is how much you mean to me
You gave life to a brand new me

You know how hard it can be, to still believe in me?
When everything I say turns to my enemy
I seek my past to place your blame
I Was not meant to be a Master

Am I awake or is this my dream?
That you've come for me
I am the God of my own History
I still believe that you will come for me

Know how hard it can be, to still believe in me?
When everything I say turns to my enemy
I seek my past to place your blame
I Was not meant to be a Master

I'll cross the highest mountain
I'll swim the endless seas
Wherever my journey will take me
The message is the same

You know how hard it can be, to still believe in me?
When everything I say turns to my enemy
I seek my past to place your blame
I Was not meant to be a Master

The song of myself is coming to an end
The words of the poet have lost its spells
This song the angels sing, your spell that caused my love
This Song of Myself has come to an end

XXVI: The Walking Shadow

The child is sitting there alone
In the darkness.
Hidden away from the Evil and War
Is she the walking shadow?

The magic flows through her fingers
She is the Child of Time
She has never felt more by herself
And now she must save them all again

Her mother died for nothing
Her father is trapped in the shadows
The child cannot trust any other
Than her own solid mind

XXVII: The Swing of Death

Because I could not feel your love
It kindly did love me
Love and heart are everywhere
Yet not a drop to me

One afternoon I said to myself
'Why isn't God more powerless?'
Does the God of love make you shiver?
Why am I so afraid?

How happy is the blood red rose?
Does it make you shiver?
I see a future with you
Why am I so afraid?

I prefer to be unhappy, for you
Rather than being alone, without you
Adoratio permanebit quotiens me eges adero
Nothing last forever, but you, you do

A fondness, however hard it tries
Will always be my undoing
The fondness talked about the future
And tore it away again

XXVIII: Three Haikus

1. Pen

Pacific nighttime
A ballpoint tiny pen writes
Out of blood

2. The Wolf

Hearty summertime
A hungry furry wolf plays
With her little ball

3. The Box

Dampen eventide
A little joyful box soars
Because of the rock

XXIX: The Sound of Fear

You will be alone now
And you are very bad at that
Your heart will fill with anger
Your mind will fill with hate

Do not waste your tears on me, my old friend
The only thing I will miss is you
We go back longer than anyone
A Tale as old as time

The Twilight Realm
Cries tears of blood
I am not giving up, but letting go
I finally believe I am fine

Do not waste your tears on me, my old friend
At least we got to say goodbye
You are going to be furious
You are going to be sad

You cannot let this turn you into a monster
Again
I am not asking for a favour. I am giving you an order
As your Queen
Do not waste your tears on me, my old friend
I will not awake, to the Sound of Fear
Of what you have done next
I Finally Believe I am okay

Xxx: The Final Frontier

Darkness fell over the universe
The War to end all Wars
Humanity's evil, clear as day
And everyone else would fall

300 planets they conquered
300 races enslaved
Stories of Hatred and Murder
Genocide sorrow and pain

The universe filled with the unknown
Behind every asteroid field
Humanity wanted to explore
Developing ships made for time

Technology can really be helpful
Technology can really be cruel
Fighting the war of time
Killing whatever remain

A beautiful race called Rumaka
With a tale as old as Time
Decided to fight the humans
Unaware of the weapon of Man

Their spectacular planet Ravena
With civilizations and stories of fame
Will burn to the end of time
As Humans slaughter their mind